Wild Animals

This book belongs to:

____

By Glorya Phillips

Mouse

Camel

Crocodile

Deer

Snake

Bear

Cheetah

Cougar

Jaguar

Tiger

Lion

Lynxes

Rhino

Elephant

Hippopotamus

Wolf

Squirrel

Monkey

Giraffe

Kangaroo

Gorilla

Ferret

Ermine

Hedgehog

Thank you for choosing us.
We hope you enjoyed our book.
Your feedback is important to us, please let us know how you like our book at:

 glorya.phillips@gmail.com

 www.facebook.com/glorya.phillips

 www.instagram.com/gloryaphillips

9 787081 195511